Anonymous

World's Columbian Exposition Art Portfolio

Anonymous

World's Columbian Exposition Art Portfolio

ISBN/EAN: 9783337859718

Printed in Europe, USA, Canada, Australia, Japan

Cover: Foto ©Thomas Meinert / pixelio.de

More available books at **www.hansebooks.com**

WORLD'S · COLVMBIAN · EXPOSITION ·
ART · PORTFOLIO

ADMINISTRATION BUILDING.
Comprising 1.6 Acres

Size, 262 x 262 Feet

Cost, $1,500,000

MUSIC HALL.   PERISTYLE   CASINO.

UPPER GRAND BASIN

MANUFACTURES AND LIBERAL ARTS BUILDING
Comprising 31 Acres.

Size. 787 x 1687 Feet

Size, 399 x 386 Feet

WOMAN'S BUILDING

Comprises 1.8 Acres.

Cost, $138,000

Size. 492 x 846 Feet.   PALACE OF MECHANICAL ARTS.   Cost, $1,200,000.
                                Comprising 9.6 Acres.

Size, 350 x 700 Feet.

MINES AND MINING BUILDING
Comprising 5.6 Acres.

Cost, $265,000

AGRICULTURAL BUILDING

Comprising 9.2 Acres

Size. 500 x 800 Feet.

Cost $618,000

Size, 250 x 998 Feet.   **HORTICULTURAL BUILDING.**   Cost, $325,000
Comprising 5.7 Acres.

PALACE OF FINE ARTS
Comprising 4.0 Acres

Size 200 x 500 Feet

Cost $670,000

BUILDING OF ELECTRICITY AND ELECTRICAL APPLIANCE
Comprising 5.5 Acres.

Size. 345 x 690 feet

Cost. $401,000

FISHERIES BUILDING
Comprising 14 Acres

Cost. $224,000

Size. 165 x 365 Feet

TRANSPORTATION BUILDING
Comprising 5.6 Acres

Size. 265 x 960 Feet.

Cost. $370,000

www.ingramcontent.com/pod-product-compliance
Lightning Source LLC
Chambersburg PA
CBHW021612270326
41931CB00009B/1448